# JESUS AIN'T WOKE

Your Guide to Real Christianity

KADE YOUNG

## JesusAintWoke.com

Copyright © 2021 by Kade Young

All rights reserved. No part of this book may be reproduced in any form by an electronic or mechanical means, including information storage and retrieval systems, without permission in writing from the copyright owner, except by a reviewer who may quote brief passages in a review.

Questions or bulk orders? Contact books@kadeyoung.com

ISBN (Paperback): 978-1-7377322-0-4
ISBN (Hardback): 978-1-7377322-2-8
ISBN (eBook): 978-1-7377322-1-1
ISBN (Audio Book): 978-1-7377322-3-5

Printed in the United States of America

Scripture quotations marked NLT are taken from the Holy Bible, New Living Translation, copyright © 1996, 2004, 2015 by Tyndale House Foundation. Used by permission of Tyndale House Publishers, Inc., Carol Stream, Illinois 60188. All rights reserved. Scripture quotations marked NKJV are taken from the New King James Version®. Copyright © 1982 by Thomas Nelson. Used by permission. All rights reserved.

# CONTENTS

Introduction: The Story Behind This Book ............................ 5

1  Woke Christianity ............................................................... 9

2  Keep On Sinning ............................................................... 13

3  The Attack on Children .................................................... 19

4  God Privilege .................................................................... 27

5  Our Secret Weapon .......................................................... 33

6  Receive God's Power ........................................................ 41

   Bonus Resources .............................................................. 45

## INTRODUCTION
# The Story Behind This Book

God set aside an entire decade to prepare me for this book.

It all began when I was led to start a blog to teach churches how to create great sound. My friends and family thought it was crazy until it started to gain momentum. Collaborate Worship now continues to reach more than 200,000 people every year.

This is nothing short of a miracle. I'm the guy who struggled in English class. I hated writing, and my teacher hated to read my writing.

Nevertheless, the blog is a success. But only because God blesses it as a result of my obedience to His unexpected assignment.

Six years later, I was hiking the trail I forged in the wooded area behind my house. Out of nowhere, God's vision for my church seemed to download into my spirit. I sensed the pastoral mantle being put on me.

Although my dad was pastoring the church at the time, he had been ready to pass it to the next leader for years. Many assumed I was next in line, but I didn't think so.

How could I be a pastor? I wasn't even thirty yet. With a man bun on the top of my head, I sure didn't look like a pastor. As a blogger and worship leader, I sure didn't act like a pastor.

While all these thoughts were running through my head, I sensed the Spirit of God ask, *"Who said I want you to pastor like someone else?"*

The question stunned me. I couldn't come up with a good answer. I felt like I had no other choice but to answer the call. So, with a bit of hesitation in my voice, I said, *"Okay. I'll do it."*

I reached out to my dad, told him about my experience, and he shouted for joy! He would have handed the church over to me that day, but I talked him into taking six months to transition so the church wouldn't go into shock.

The time came for me to officially take the lead. It was now up to me to prepare a message for the church every single week. Talk about a daunting task!

I had preached a few times here and there, and it was always exhausting. Preparation felt like going to the dentist, and the delivery was always a bit disappointing.

Now that I was the lead pastor, I thought I'd be suffering through this same experience every single week. To my surprise, the first few messages came much easier than expected. It seemed like a fluke, but it continued to be a challenging yet pleasant experience.

God gave me a grace I didn't have before. Preparing messages quickly became my favorite weekly assignment. And all the people who were worried about having to suffer through my sermons began to realize they were actually enjoying them.

What's interesting is the way God led me to prepare. I would write out the entire message. I would then read my transcript word for word in front of the church.

Although some use this method, it is rare and usually frowned upon in the modern church. Yet, I knew this was the method God wanted me to use. Now I know why.

Two hundred blog posts and ninety sermons later, I've written enough to fill more than five novels.

It wasn't until my second year of pastoring that I began to realize that writing is the primary way I am called to serve those around me. Thanks to Jordan Raynor's book, Master of One, I discovered that the many things I was doing all had one thread: writing.

Then I began to ponder the idea of authoring a book, and it resonated. I knew it was something I was supposed to do. But when? And what was the book God wanted me to write first?

I didn't know, so I waited. Sometimes patiently. Sometimes not.

About a year went by when my wife and I visited a church we had never been to. I knew the pastor because he was one of my Rhema instructors ten years before, but he didn't know me.

Out of nowhere, in the middle of the service, Pastor Jay Hoskins walked up to me, put his hand on my shoulder, and quietly said, *"You are going to write books, and people will read them,"* and then quickly walked off to continue his message.

Although we had recently reconnected because his church was subleasing our church building, he didn't know me from Adam. The only person that knew I wanted to author a book was my wife. So, needless to say, this word of knowledge fueled the holy fire within me.

But I still didn't know what book to write. I didn't want to write a book just to write a book. I wanted to write a book that God wanted me to write. So, once again, I waited.

Another year goes by. My wife occasionally asks when I will write a book, and I remind her I am waiting on God to tell me what book to write.

Then, one random day, I am in my office praying and seeking God as I do most every morning. Only this time, I had a vision. It was a book cover. The book I saw in the vision is exactly the book you are reading.

So, read on. This is not my book. This is God's book. And I know without a doubt, He is going to use it to lead countless people to freedom in Jesus Christ.

# 1
# Woke Christianity

The term "woke" has pure beginnings. In the 1930s, "stay woke" simply meant to pay attention to the social and political issues that impacted racial equality.

It has since been hijacked as the rallying cry for identity politics where politicians target minority groups for political gain by posing as their ally.

Now, to be "woke," you must:
- Advocate for the LGBTQ+ movement by allowing men to be women and drag queens to teach your kids in school.
- Fuel the racial wildfire by defunding the police and making sure white people are viewed as "privileged."
- Support Critical Race Theory where white children are told to apologize for their race.

The list goes on, but you get the idea.

The challenge is, on the surface, these issues seem to have good intentions. But dig deeper, and you'll find out that almost everything "woke" is anti-God. Yet Christians everywhere are becoming "woke" in the name of "love."

For example, we're told that to love the LGBTQ+ community, we must advocate for their cause. Never mind the fact that God has made clear that everything the community stands for is sin.

But hey, we're supposed to love them, right? Yet, the love chapter in the Bible tells us that love does not rejoice in iniquity but rejoices in the truth. (1 Cor 13:6) How do we get around that?

I know. We'll adopt the world's definition of love: Love is inclusion and acceptance.

## THE GOD OF INCLUSION

The American church is intimidated by culture's demand for inclusion, so we forsake God's commands and worship the god of inclusion instead.

It's not that we've believed an outright lie; we would be able to recognize that. But we've adopted a half-truth, which is not truth at all.

The truth is, Christianity does not exclude people; it excludes sin. And sin isn't defined by Christians. It's defined by the most read book of all time: the Bible.

What this means is that people exclude themselves from Christianity by choosing to keep on sinning instead of letting

Jesus take away their sin. And most of the time, it's because the church willingly neglected its duty to confront sin with truth and love.

As a result, some people think they belong to God when they don't. Because of their sin, they sense a need for freedom and think they will find it in getting others to accept their sin.

**But freedom is only found when you let Jesus *take away your sin.***

Are you starting to get uncomfortable? Don't put the book down just yet because I will show you the path to freedom.

# 2
# Keep On Sinning

The American church was once guilty of legalism. You were judged for how you looked and where you came from.

Thankfully, most recognized the error and began a course correction. Grace became the poster child of the church. Forgiveness and acceptance were the focus of almost every message.

It's almost like sin didn't matter anymore. You could now be a Christian without worrying about changing your lifestyle... or at least that's what people thought.

That's what I thought. As a kid, the message I got from church was, "God loves you no matter what. Don't worry about those things you feel guilty about. God still loves you."

And it's true! God's love is not tied to our behavior. It is unconditional. He loves us from the moment we are formed in the womb, and His love never stops.

The challenge is, God's love does not ignore sin.

**God's love confronts sin.**

## WHY GOD HATES SIN

Sin is an enemy of God. Why? It kills His children. It steals their joy. It destroys their life.

That's why God sent Jesus not only to forgive sin but to take away sin. (1 John 3:5) He is a warrior for righteousness because freedom from sin enables us to get close to God. That's what Jesus wants: relationship.

**But He can't take away our sin if we keep holding onto it.**

As a teenager, I found myself in bondage to the hyper-grace teaching of the church. I thought sin wasn't a big deal, that God overlooked it and understood if I chose to keep it around.

So, I kept it around. It felt good. It was fun. I made new friends because of my sin. On top of it all, many would agree that I was born that way and would always be that way.

Yep, you guessed it. My sin of choice was homosexuality.

I hid it from my parents. I hid it from my church. After all, they never really talked about sin, only that God loved me regardless. So, I figured they didn't need to know anyway.

Only one problem. I was in bondage, and I knew it.

When emotions were high, and adrenaline was flowing, it was all fun and games. But when I was by myself, my soul was crying out for freedom. But how could I need freedom from something that was covered by the grace of God?

## KEEP ON SINNING

You see, no one told me that those who keep on sinning only prove they belong to the devil. (1 John 3:8) This is a scripture we conveniently ignore so it doesn't get in the way of attracting more people to our church.

But what if this truth holds power to set people free? It does. Because the rest of the verse goes on to say, *"But the son of God came to destroy the works of the devil."*

When we say yes to Jesus, we are born into God's family. And those who are in God's family don't make a practice of sinning because God's life is in them.

In other words, you can't keep on sinning when you are truly a child of God. (1 John 3:9)

These are the kind of statements, even though taken directly from the Bible, that will get you accused of having a religious spirit. Why? Because it feels like your parents just showed up to shut down the secret party.

And you know what? Jesus already shut down the party when He revealed that there will be people on judgment day who think they are saved, only to find out they're not.

It's not a mystery who these people are because Jesus tells us how to know if you are really saved. He says, *"Only those who actually do the will of my Father in heaven will enter the kingdom of heaven."* (Matthew 7:21)

Wait a minute. I thought salvation was a free gift? That it

wasn't attached to my behavior, and all I had to do was believe?

This is true! Salvation can't be earned. It is a free gift only obtained by faith in Jesus Christ. But here's the deal:

**When you believe in Jesus, you follow Jesus.**

WHAT YOU BELIEVE, YOU FOLLOW

I've never met a football fan who doesn't follow their favorite team. Even if the team is losing, they drop everything to watch the game. They pay loads of money to wear the gear and travel to the games. They take off work; they skip church. Whatever it takes.

So, I'll say it again. When you believe in Jesus, you follow Jesus.

Following Jesus, also known as doing the will of the Father, is not something you do to earn salvation. It's what you do because you've been saved.

The reality is, it's easy to tell who are children of God and who are children of the devil. Those who keep on sinning, even if they claim to be a Christian, belong to the devil. But those who daily seek to do the will of the Father, even though not perfect, are children of God.

I'll be honest. I was a child of the devil even when I thought I was a Christian. I was even leading worship for my youth group as a child of the devil.

But I got tired of being in bondage. I was tired of the church telling me it was okay. I wanted freedom, and I was going to get it no matter what it took.

Let me tell you, when you start seeking freedom, Jesus will give it to you even when the church won't.

## FREE FROM SIN

I received complete freedom from homosexuality in my bedroom as I was crying out to God to not just forgive me but to take it away from me. And He did.

That day, Jesus became not just my savior but my Lord. I received more than forgiveness of sin; I received freedom from sin and the power I needed to stay away from it.

My wife of fourteen years and my four beautiful kids are a living testimony of what God can do when you truly believe in the power of Jesus to take away your sin.

Lest you think that I never struggled again after the day I was delivered, you need to know that I did. There were still thoughts that had to be overcome and habits that had to be broken.

Although it wasn't a walk in the park, after the encounter when Jesus took away my sin, I never committed the act again. Temptation continued to rear its ugly head, but there was a newfound power inside of me to overcome it. It was the power of Jesus.

**This is how true Christianity deals with sin. We expose it and invite Jesus to take it away. And by faith, we are set free.**

But Woke Christianity keeps sin in the shadows and even goes so far as to advocate for sin. Here's what it sounds like:

*"We can't confront sin at church because the sinner will feel excluded."*

That statement sounds so right. We even pat ourselves on the back as we gloat in our ability to make sinners feel welcome in our church services.

This has been going on in the church for years, and what is the result?

Families are more broken than ever. Biblical morals have corroded to where they have almost disappeared. All this happened while the church was having its party.

## LET JESUS TAKE AWAY YOUR SIN

Have you believed the lie that you can keep on sinning and pretend to belong to God? There's no better time than now to invite Jesus to take away your sin.

After all, **when you believe in Jesus, you follow Jesus.**

# 3
# The Attack on Children

"When a Man Loves a Woman" is a very well-known song for a reason. It explains exactly how God designed marriage.

When a man loves a woman, he leaves his old life behind to become one with his wife. A sacred relationship is established when the man enters into his wife and the two become one flesh.

Leave it up to God to make this the most pleasurable experience we have on the earth. And as if that is not enough, He rewards us for being intimate: divine multiplication. Yes, I'm talking about children.

Marriage is a gift from God. Children are a gift from God. It's no mystery why these two things are always under attack.

But when it comes down to it, the enemy only hates one thing: humankind.

We were made in God's image. So when Satan sees us, he sees

God. Needless to say, he is jealous of us.

## WHAT THE ENEMY HATES MOST

Satan doesn't just hate Christians; he hates everyone. He wants us all dead. Yet God gave us this amazing ability to multiply.

So, what do you think Satan is after most? Our children. He must stop the multiplication.

Let's examine how he does this:
- Destroy God's design for the family so everyone is unfulfilled and broken.
- Create a culture where children are a nuisance so people don't want to have kids and push aside the ones they do have.
- Make society numb to killing babies through abortion.
- Normalize food and drugs that ruin the reproductive system.
- Promote homosexuality so reproduction is impossible.

Shall I go on?

**The challenges we're up against all lead to one thing: the destruction of children.**

What's worse is, the woke church plays along.

It starts innocently by kicking kids out of the main service so they can't distract from the message. After all, kids are a nuisance, right?

Then the pastor stops talking about God's design for marriage and family. After all, this is a sensitive subject and we don't want anyone to feel excluded, right?

Abortion is definitely not going to be talked about because the woke church would rather bow to the god of inclusion than admit that abortion is murder.

## THE "BIG" SINS

The Christians that dare to talk about these issues get accused of focusing too much on the "big" sins: abortion and homosexuality. They say, *"Sin is sin. And if you talk about one, you have to talk about them all equally."*

Before they shut you down too, let me explain why this accusation is nonsense.

In the culture we live in, abortion is being pitched as a woman's right. Homosexuality has its own advocacy group to make sure everyone sees it as normal sexual expression. If you look at culture's definition, neither abortion nor homosexuality is a sin.

But what about other sins, like rape or murder? They don't yet have an advocacy group trying to convince the public it's okay. Christians and non-christians agree; both of these are bad and even deserve punishment.

**As Christians, we are advocates of righteousness.**

When Satan tries to destroy culture with normalized sin, we issue a counterattack and expose sin so we can lead people to freedom in Jesus Christ.

The woke church makes sin comfortable so everyone feels included. Jesus' church makes sin uncomfortable so people recognize their need for a savior.

But wait. Doesn't the Bible say not to judge? That's a scripture even unbelievers know by heart.

But how do you explain when Jesus said, *"Do not judge according to appearance, but judge with righteous judgment."* (John 7:24)

Now we are in a pickle. The Bible tells us not to judge, yet here, Jesus is telling us how to judge. To figure this out, let's take a look at the most popular misunderstood scripture of all time:

*"Do not judge anyone, anytime, for any reason."* -Not Jesus

That's how we like to quote it, but Jesus really said, *"Judge not, that you be not judged."* (Matthew 7:1)

From this one isolated scripture, I can see how people think Jesus is telling us not to judge anyone, anytime, for any reason. But Jesus wasn't done talking yet. Let's see what else He has to say.

*"For with what judgment you judge, you will be judged; and with the measure you use, it will be measured back to you."* (Matthew 7:2)

Okay. Now the picture is starting to come into focus. If I decide to judge someone else, I better be prepared to receive the same kind of judgment in return. Jesus uses an example to help us understand:

*"And why do you look at the speck in your brother's eye, but do not consider the plank in your own eye?"* (Matthew 7:3-4)

To understand scripture, it's crucial to know who it was written to. At first, it seems like Jesus is talking to everyone. It seems like He's saying, *"Nobody judge anyone so we can all live our own lives without making people upset."*

But Jesus wasn't giving this instruction to everyone. He was talking to a specific group of people: hypocrites. He even calls them by name:

*"Hypocrite! First remove the plank from your own eye, and then you will see clearly to remove the speck from your brother's eye."* (Matthew 7:5)

Whoops. Maybe I should have edited out that second part. I mean, since we are not supposed to judge, we can't have Jesus telling us it's okay to remove the speck from our brother's eye.

Now that we've heard everything he had to say, we now know that Jesus is saying, *"Hey, hypocrites! Since you don't want to judge yourself, stop judging others."*

The problem is, hypocrites don't know how to stop judging others. It's how they make themselves feel good about their own mess.

## RIGHTEOUS JUDGMENT

But, there is a way to judge with righteous judgment. First, judge yourself. Am I pursuing God's will? Am I doing what God asked me to do? Am I obedient to the Word of God?

**Once you establish self-judgment, you are ready to help someone else out of their mess.**

You know you're ready when your mindset has shifted. You used to point out someone else's mess to feel better about your mess. But now, you only point out someone else's mess to lead them to the same freedom you have.

The woke method of ignoring and even celebrating sin only leads to destruction. The Jesus method of judging with righteous judgment will help you lead others to salvation.

## DESTROYING THE WORKS OF THE DEVIL

It's time to issue a counterattack. We can't just sit back while the enemy destroys our children.

We must confront the progressive sexual agenda and re-establish God's design for sex: one man and one woman committed to each other in marriage.

The best place to start? Our schools. Parents need to stand up and speak out against woke sex education and establish curriculum that teaches God's design for sex.

We must put a stop to abortion by making it known that it is not a woman's right. It is murder. Let's vote for government officials who will stop being passive about the slaughter of innocent children and pass laws that put a stop to it.

Most of all, we must start valuing children as the gift they are. They are not in the way. They are not a nuisance. They are a blessing from God.

## PARENTS: YOU WERE MADE FOR THIS

Is it a challenge to raise kids? Yes. But parents, you were made for this. God has equipped you to not just survive until you become an empty nester, but to mentor your children to become mind-blowing men and women of God.

**Your kids are meant to walk with you through life, not be pushed aside while you live your life.**

There's no better time than now to invite your kids to go with you on the amazing journey ahead.

# 4
# God Privilege

I don't know if you've seen my picture or not, but I would definitely be categorized as white. Although, if you want to get technical, I am a mix of many different races. I even have enough Cherokee Indian blood to be considered part of the tribe.

That's beside the point, though. As far as woke folks are concerned, I am a white male, and they aren't very happy about it.

In my early twenties, I went to work for a church that had a predominantly black congregation. For the first time in my life, I was the minority in the room.

Growing up, I vividly remember my mom teaching me that we never treat people differently because of their skin color. As a kid, it made total sense. So I fully embraced this truth.

I've recently discovered that, by default, kids don't care about skin color. My five-year-old daughter saw a black man with the same body type and beard length as me and said, *"Daddy, he looks just like you!"*

Even though skin color isn't something I think about, I'll admit that the first few days at the new job, it felt strange to be the minority. I was the only white guy in the office.

It only took a few days to get over the shock of a new environment before realizing what a gift it was to emerge in a culture other than my own.

Every time we had lunch at the church, the sweet ladies in the kitchen would bring food to my office. And let me tell ya, it was some good cookin'! They were always worried that I was too skinny, so they would bring me more than one dessert and expect me to eat it all.

I only remember one negative race-related experience in the three years I worked there. A woman came into the main office, peeked into mine on the way to the secretary, and started yelling, *"You mean to tell me we hired a WHITE BOY!?"*

I didn't know if I should hide or run away. But the secretary, who is still a dear friend of mine, did a tremendous job handling the situation, and we moved on without bringing it up again.

Several years after I had moved on from this job, I reconnected with one of my coworkers there. It was an election year, so, of course, race was being exploited for political gain. She saw a Facebook post of mine that hit a nerve, so she wanted to talk about it.

We hopped on the phone, and she started the conversation with, *"Kade, the time we spent working together made me realize that not all white people are racist. I was expecting you to slip up, and you never did. So, I know, without a doubt, you aren't racist."*

This statement shocked me because she always did a great job hiding her suspicions. I never knew that I was under trial. But I am so thankful God used me to help her overcome these challenges.

Growing up, she had been taught to look out for white people, and for a good reason. The history between whites and blacks is very troubling. My compassion runs deep for those who have been hurt by the evil of racism.

But if we step back and take an honest look at the tension between blacks and whites, we'll find that the enemy works to stir up the peaceful waters and turn the tables every time we are on the verge of resolve.

We're deceived into elevating one race over the other. On the surface, it seems like a solid solution. But think a little deeper, and you'll realize that **equality can never exist when one is elevated over the other.**

The woke church helps the enemy advance his agenda. They proudly wear their race-elevating gear to church and go home feeling really good about themselves.

IS IT GODLY?

This is a good place to pause and show you how to know if

what you are doing is godly or not.

Do your actions elevate you, or do they elevate God? If you go home patting yourself on the back, you can be sure it had nothing to do with God.

A good example is the people who bow down to the god of racism by publicly apologizing for being white. Then they walk off with a smile on their face because they feel so good about what they just did.

Let me clear this up for you. That's called worshiping an idol. The woke church may be encouraging it, but Jesus' church stays far from it.

## CRITICAL RACE THEORY

This idol expresses itself in many ways, one of which being Critical Race Theory (CRT).

Notice it's a theory, which means it is an idea. Legal scholars developed the idea to examine racism in the legal system—definitely a worthy cause. If racism is built into our legal structures, I think we all agree that it needs to be found and dealt with.

But CRT has been hijacked by the enemy.

It is now being used as a racial weapon in our public schools. Teachers who bow to the god of racism "teach" Critical Race Theory thinking they are doing a service, but all they accomplish is turning students against each other.

White kids leave class feeling ashamed of their race. Everyone else leaves upset with their "privileged" white friends.

## WHITE PRIVILEGE

This reveals the next expression of the racism idol: white privilege. Yet another theory (idea) that white people have the upper hand in life simply because they are white. Go ahead and prove that idea to all the white people struggling to get by. I'll wait.

Have you ever noticed how people look for ways to put down those who are more successful?

"It's because they have rich parents."

"It's because they don't pay their employees enough."

"It's because they are white."

The reality is, there will always be someone who was dealt a better hand in life than you. They have more resources. They are more talented. They have better connections.

But the only person you are responsible for is you. When you get to heaven, God is not going to ask you how someone else used their talents. He's going to ask how you used yours.

God is not impressed by those who have the most. He's impressed with those who multiply what they have. (Matthew 25)

White privilege is not a part of the solution. It's a distraction.

So, what is the solution?

## THE SOLUTION

In the book of Romans, you'll find the Apostle Paul working hard to disarm racial tensions between the Jews and the Gentiles. Interestingly, he addresses the issue of the Jews being privileged and the Gentiles not.

Instead of trying to make the Jews feel bad about their privileged status, he invites the Gentiles to become part of it. He says, *"Because of our faith, Christ has brought us into this place of undeserved privilege where we now stand."* Romans 5:2

This is what I like to call "God Privilege," and it's available to all who believe in Jesus Christ—no matter their race.

The woke church doesn't want anyone to be privileged. But Jesus' church seeks to walk in God Privilege and help others do the same.

This is the answer to racism. Instead of teaching others about Critical Race Theory and White Privilege, we must focus on leading people to Jesus and making it known that God Privilege is available to all who believe.

God Privilege is available to me, and it's available to you. So are you going to keep griping about how life isn't fair? Or are you going to step into the promises of God and show others how to do the same?

# 5
# Our Secret Weapon

The woke church is a counterfeit. It has great influence but no power. It attracts crowds of spectators but produces no followers of Jesus. It puts on a great performance, but everyone goes home to life as usual.

**But what if the woke church woke up?**

That's exactly what is going to happen. And the revival that breaks out is going to be unlike anything that's ever been seen.

Since you've made it this far in the book, I'm going to assume you are not a part of the woke church. Maybe you never were, and you are using this book for confirmation. Or you were once "woke," and God has used this book to shake you awake.

## WELCOME TO THE REMNANT

Either way, allow me to officially welcome you to the remnant. We may be outnumbered, but don't let it scare you. God is a pro at using a small group of people to accomplish great things.

But He does need our cooperation. Don't sit back and think that God is going to do this on His own. He could if He wanted to. But that's not how He designed it.

To accomplish things on the earth, God has to work through people. That's how He designed it.

That's why Jesus, in His last message to the disciples, said, *"He who believes in Me will do the same works I've done, and even greater works because I am going to be with the Father."* (John 14:12)

Jesus said this right after He had just explained, for the umpteenth time, that Jesus and God were one. The words Jesus spoke? God's. The miracles Jesus worked? Yep, it was God working through Him.

He wants you to understand this because it reveals that you can do what He did. And not only that, but now you can do greater things than He did.

But you can only do these things when you realize that it was the Father doing these things through Jesus. It wasn't because Jesus was super-human. It's because He fully submitted Himself to the Father.

## GOD'S POWER WORKING THROUGH YOU

It was God's power working through Jesus. Just like it can be God's power working through you.

**But you have to give God full control.**

You can't do this in your own power, just like Jesus didn't do this in His own power. He worked miracles and spoke mind-boggling truth simply because He submitted Himself to God. And Jesus wants you to do the same.

That's why the very next thing Jesus says is, *"If you ask anything in My name, I will do it."* (John 14:14)

Wow! So Jesus just invited us to work the same miracles He did. Then He took it a step further and told us to do greater things than He did. Now, He's telling us that we can ask anything and He will do it.

It seems impossible, and I guess Jesus knew we would think that, so He goes on to explain how it is possible. He says, *"If you love Me, keep My commandments. And I will pray the Father, and He will give you another Helper, that He may abide with you forever—the Spirit of truth."* (John 14:15-17 NKJV)

For clarity, Jesus reiterates the same thing just a few verses down:

*"He who has My commandments and keeps them, it is he who loves Me. And he who loves Me will be loved by My Father, and I will love him and manifest Myself to him."* (John 14:21 NKJV)

## OBEDIENCE IS REQUIRED

So now you know, obeying God is a prerequisite for seeing the power of God.

It makes total sense why we never see miracles in the woke church. **Obedience to God is not pursued but rather ignored** in the name of inclusion.

In case you are still not getting it, Jesus explains it a third time:

*"If anyone loves Me, he will keep My word; and My Father will love him, and We will come to him and make Our home with him."* (John 14:23 NKJV)

If you want the power of God to manifest in your life, just like it did through Jesus, obedience to God's Word is required.

## GRACE VS OBEDIENCE

The woke church settled for grace without obedience. And when we choose to tolerate sin in the name of grace, we dismiss the power of God. After all, the power of God cannot exist alongside disobedience. Let me put it to you this way:

**Grace without obedience invites human weakness. Obedience because of grace invites the power of God.**

After working so hard to get this across to us, Jesus reveals that living a life of obedience is going to cause the world to hate us. (John 15:19) But wait a minute... I thought we were supposed to try to get the world to like us so they would come to our church?

Well, according to Jesus, if the world loves you, it's because you belong to it. But if you belong to Jesus, you will obey His commandments. And as you walk in obedience, not only will the world hate you, but the woke church will hate you too. (John 15:18-19)

This isn't very encouraging, but Jesus reveals these things for a reason: so you won't abandon your faith when things get tough.

Persecution isn't fun. It can make you think that you are doing something wrong. But you're not. It's actually an indicator that you are doing something right. When persecution comes because of your obedience to God, be encouraged and keep moving forward.

But you will always struggle with obedience if it is coming from the wrong place.

## PERFORMANCE VS IDENTITY

By default, obedience is a performance. We learn it at a young age. To avoid negative consequences, we perform according to our parent's script even when our true desire is to do something else.

We carry this into our relationship with God. We perform for Him by doing our best to live according to His script. Quite often, we miss a line or two (sometimes even missing the entire act), but we always seem to find our way back into the performance.

We think God's impressed when we get it right. We think He yells at us when we get it wrong. But it turns out, God doesn't want us to perform at all.

When it came time to write this book, I set aside a few days in my schedule to go to a secluded cabin and focus. In my mind, I envisioned getting to the cabin, opening my computer, and writing nonstop until the book was done. But that's not what happened.

I started the day like normal, getting quiet before the Lord. After prayer and reading His Word, I said, "Alright Holy Spirit, you ready to write this book?" To my surprise, the answer was no.

I knew that I needed to spend more time being quiet and listening to His instructions. Only, He wasn't giving me instructions other than to be quiet.

I sat on the back deck for a while and watched the trees. Then I laid on the deck for a while and closed my eyes. I did my best to eliminate thoughts of guilt for not producing anything while my wife was at home caring for our four young children.

About an hour passed, and I asked again, "Ready to write this book?" The answer was still no.

So I walked down to the lake, sat on the shore, and watched the waves. I could sense the Holy Spirit nudging me to get in the water, but I didn't want to. The lake is gross.

Then I remembered my goal at the cabin was absolute obedience. So I found a clean rock to put on top of the slimy rock and sat on it in the water.

As the waves were rolling over the top of my thighs, I sensed the Holy Spirit say, *"Wave after wave of blessing is coming into your life."* I watched as the waves started small and then began to grow.

Then the Holy Spirit said, *"Look up."* I looked up and noticed the beautiful, wispy clouds in the sky. As I looked closer,

I realized that they were in the shape of three different angels. Immediately, I was reminded of the scripture, *"He shall give His angels charge over you."* (Psalm 91:11 NKJV)

After these two experiences, I was overcome with the goodness of God. I sat there in awe of who He is. I was amazed that He chose me to write this book and promised to protect me from the opposition that will come because of it.

Then I heard, *"Now you're ready. You came here to perform. I wasn't looking for a performance. I'm looking for obedience that comes as a result of knowing who you are to Me."*

For the first time in my life, I realized that obedience to God comes in one of two ways. Either you are performing, or it is an overflow of your identity in Jesus Christ.

We aren't capable of a flawless performance. But obedience comes easy when we know who we are to God.

Because of our faith in Jesus, we are made right with God. We now stand in a place of undeserved privilege and even share God's glory. (Romans 3:22, 5:2)

I could go on and on sharing scriptures about how valuable you are to God, but it would do more good for you to seek them out yourself.

And I encourage you to do so because obedience is your secret weapon. It's required for the power of God to work in your life and for you to get to a place where you can ask anything of Jesus and He will do it.

**Obedience is not something we do; it's who we are.**

When we embrace and live out this truth, the power of God is made manifest in our lives. And we won't just do the same works as Jesus; we will do greater works.

# 6
# Receive God's Power

Obedience is the prerequisite to God's power, but it's not the source of God's power. In other words, obedience is preparation. It's how we get ready for God's power to show up.

Now that we're prepared, how do we invite the power of God to show up?

This is a question the disciples were asking Jesus before He ascended into Heaven. Up until this point, Jesus was their source of God's power. But Jesus was about to leave and expected them to do greater works than He did.

Can you imagine? I bet they were begging him to stay and asking questions like, "How are we supposed to do greater things than you if you are not here to help us?"

Right before ascending into Heaven, Jesus commanded the disciples to wait. He said, *"Don't do anything yet. Wait for a few days until you are baptized with the Holy Spirit."* (Acts 1:4-5)

Then He told them why they are being baptized in the Holy Spirit. He said, *"You will receive power when the Holy Spirit comes upon you and you will be my witnesses, telling people about me everywhere."* (Acts 1:8 NLT)

## THE HOLY SPIRIT

**The Holy Spirit is the source of God's power.** Without the baptism of the Holy Spirit, we have no chance at doing the works Jesus did, much less greater works.

And now you probably realize why the baptism of the Holy Spirit is such a sensitive subject in the church. Some denominations believe in it, and others don't. The woke church simply ignores it to make sure no one gets uncomfortable.

Where can we lay the blame for so many people being sucked into the ravages of woke Christianity? Neglecting the baptism of the Holy Spirit. Why? Because the Holy Spirit is not just the power of God, He is the Spirit of truth. (John 16:13)

## THE SPIRIT OF TRUTH

Without the Holy Spirit, we have no chance of discerning truth from lies.

That's why people fall for the clever race theories. That's why people celebrate the bondage of sexual perversion. That's why people ignore the slaughter of babies. That's why people believe everything they hear on the news and live their life in fear.

There's a good chance this book exposed at least one lie you used to believe. Do you know why? The Holy Spirit is the one behind this book. I'm just the messenger.

It's only by the Holy Spirit that we can clearly see the truth.

## RECEIVE THE HOLY SPIRIT

But you don't need to rely on me to help you discern the truth. You can have the baptism of the Holy Spirit for yourself, and He will lead you into all truth and give you the power you need to lead others into the truth.

So you have a choice. You can believe all the lies you've heard about the baptism of the Holy Spirit and continue to live powerless. Or you can receive God's power right now by inviting the Holy Spirit into your life.

So, go ahead. What are you waiting for? You don't have to wait for a church service where the pastor invites people to receive the Holy Spirit.

**You can be baptized in the Holy Spirit right where you are. He's just waiting for you to ask.**

BONUS RESOURCE

# Filled with the Holy Spirit

A free online course to guide you in your relationship with the Holy Spirit.

Get access today at
**JesusAintWoke.com**

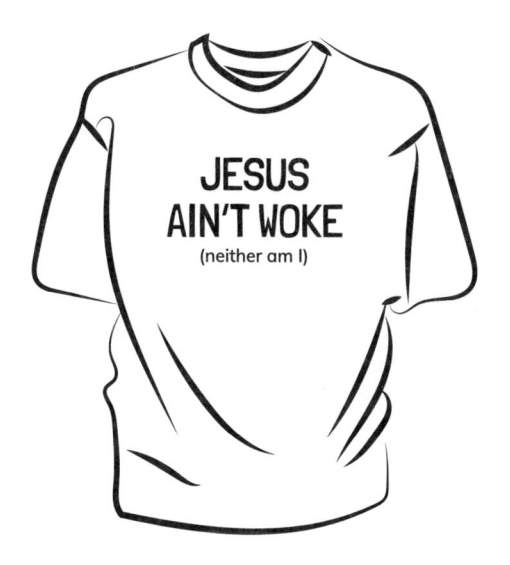

## BONUS RESOURCES

**JESUS AIN'T WOKE**
(neither am I)

Get your gear at
**JesusAintWoke.com**

# Let's lead people to true freedom in Jesus.

Ask the Holy Spirit to show you one person who needs this book.

Order books at
**JesusAintWoke.com**

# Can we text you helpful resources?

Join our texting list and we will help you lead people to true freedom in Jesus.

Text **Ain't woke** to
1-833-877-1237